**Senior Art Editor** Anna Formanek
**Project Editor** Lara Hutcheson
**Managing Editor** Tori Kosara
**Managing Art Editor** Jo Connor
**Designer** Emma Wicks
**Production Editor** Siu Yin Chan
**Senior Production Controller** Lloyd Robertson
**Publisher** Paula Regan
**Art Director** Charlotte Coulais
**Managing Director** Mark Searle

**Written by** Lara Hutcheson
**Designed for DK by** Thelma-Jane Robb
**Reading Consultant** Barbara Marinak

DK would like to thank Hank Woon, Alyssa Tuffey, and the rest of the team at The Pokémon Company International. Thanks also to Lori Hand for proofreading.

First American Edition, 2025
Published in the United States by DK Publishing,
a division of Penguin Random House LLC
1745 Broadway, 20th Floor, New York, NY 10019
25 26 27 28 29 10 9 8 7 6 5 4 3 2 1
001–344860–Jul/2025

© 2025 Pokémon. © 1997–2023 Nintendo, Creatures, GAME FREAK,
TV Tokyo, ShoPro, JR Kikaku. TM, ® Nintendo.

All rights reserved.
Without limiting the rights under the copyright reserved above, no part of this publication may be reproduced, stored in or introduced into a retrieval system, or transmitted, in any form, or by any means (electronic, mechanical, photocopying, recording, or otherwise), without the prior written permission of the copyright owner.
Published in Great Britain by Dorling Kindersley Limited

A catalog record for this book
is available from the Library of Congress.
ISBN 978-0-5939-6582-5 (Paperback)
ISBN 978-0-5939-6583-2 (Hardcover)

DK books are available at special discounts when purchased
in bulk for sales promotions, premiums, fund-raising, or educational use.
For details, contact: DK Publishing Special Markets,
1745 Broadway, 20th Floor, New York, NY 10019
SpecialSales@dk.com

Printed and bound in China

www.dk.com
www.pokemon.com

This book was made with Forest Stewardship Council™ certified paper—one small step in DK's commitment to a sustainable future.
Learn more at
www.dk.com/uk/information/sustainability

Level 2

# Pokémon
## Ready, Set, Catch!

DK

# Contents

| | |
|---|---|
| 6 | Catching Pokémon |
| 8 | Friede's team |
| 10 | Finding Pokémon |
| 12 | Wild Pokémon |
| 14 | Poké Balls |
| 16 | Be prepared |
| 18 | Rotom Phone |
| 20 | Battle time |
| 22 | Know your types |
| 24 | Winning moves |
| 26 | Perfect partners |
| 28 | Never give up |
| 30 | Glossary |
| 31 | Index |
| 32 | Quiz |

# Catching Pokémon

Pokémon Trainers like to catch lots of Pokémon. They hope to make a strong team.

The strongest teams will often include Pokémon that have a range of different skills in battle.

Pokémon Trainer, Spinel

**Beheeyem**

Beheeyem can control opponents' memories.

**Umbreon**

Umbreon has a powerful battle move called "Snarl."

# Friede's team

Friede's team includes Captain Pikachu and Charizard. They are always happy to help each other out.

**Working together**

Captain Pikachu helps Friede on the airship, *The Brave Olivine*.

**Catch a ride**

Friede can travel on Charizard's back.

**Brave and fierce**

Together the team is strong in battle.

## Finding Pokémon

Pokémon can be found in all sorts of places.

Some Pokémon like to come out at night, while others prefer the day.

Sunflora enjoy the sunshine. It gives them energy.

Eyes can see in the dark

Noctowl like to come out at night.

**Places to look for Pokémon**
- Forests and fields
- Lakes and seas
- Caves
- Trees

# Wild Pokémon

Would you like to catch a wild Pokémon?

They are found all over the Pokémon world, if you know where to look for them!

### Finding Combee

Look for Combee near flowers. They like to gather nectar.

### Forest friends

You can find Jumpluff, Skiddo, and Venomoth in Arboliva's Forest.

Some Poké Balls are better at catching certain Pokémon than others.

A good Trainer knows which Poké Ball to use.

## Be prepared

Sometimes a Poké Ball isn't the only thing you need to be able to catch Pokémon.

Ludlow and his fishing rod.

A fishing rod can be used to catch Pokémon in the water.

You can also use tasty berries and snacks to tempt Pokémon out from hiding.

**Finding berries makes Chansey happy.**

# Rotom Phone

The Rotom Phone is a useful device. It includes a Pokédex.

A Pokédex is packed with facts about Pokémon.

**Rotom Phone can:**

- Identify a Pokémon
- Give their height, weight, and type
- Provide facts about their habitat and needs
- Tell you about their battle style

Rotom Phone

Liko and Roy were given a Rotom Phone at the start of their Pokémon journey.

**On screen**

This Rotom Phone is showing a Pokémon called Doliv.

## Battle time

Pokémon are easier to catch if they are weakened first in battle.

They only want to be caught by a strong Trainer!

Liko wants to be brave in battle.

**Sprigatito vs. Galarian Moltres**

Liko's Sprigatito used a battle move called Leafage to calm Galarian Moltres.

# Know your types

In battle, it is good to know what types of Pokémon are strong or weak against others.

Golduck

Sharp claws

Webbed feet

A Water type, like Golduck, can be strong against a Fire type, like Slugma.

# Winning moves

Rock types, like Sudowoodo, are often strong against Fire types, like Fuecoco.

**Sudowoodo's Rock Throw**

This Rock-type move caught Roy and Fuecoco by surprise!

**Worn out**

Fuecoco did its best, but it was beaten in battle.

**Roy's regret**

Roy wished he had known more about his opponent.

## Perfect partners

Not all Pokémon are hard to catch. Dot chose her friend Quaxly to be her first Pokémon.

They did not have to battle because Quaxly was very happy to be chosen.

**Dot and Quaxly**

**Dot's Poké Ball**

**Catching Quaxly**

When Dot threw her Poké Ball, Quaxly jumped right in.

# Never give up

There are so many amazing Pokémon to discover. Keep on searching.

Build a top Pokémon team and get ready for your next adventure!

**Friends together**

# Glossary

**Device**
An invention or machine used for a special purpose.

**Habitat**
The natural environment of an animal or plant.

**Nectar**
Sweet liquid found in flowers.

**Opponent**
Someone who is competing against another.

**Poké Ball**
A ball used by Trainers to catch and carry Pokémon.

**Pokémon Trainer**
Someone who raises Pokémon and battles with them in competition.

**Tempt**
To make someone want to do something.

# Index

**A**
Ancient Poké Ball  15
Arboliva's Forest  13

**B**
Beheeyem  7
*The Brave Olivine*  8

**C**
Captain Pikachu  8
Chansey  17
Charizard  8-9
Combee  13

**D**
Doliv  19
Dot  26-27

**F**
Fire type  23, 24-25
Friede  8-9
Fuecoco  24-25

**G**
Galarian Moltres  21
Golduck  22-23
Great Ball  15

**J**
Jumpluff  12-13

**L**
Leafage  21
Liko  19, 20-21
Ludlow  16

**M**
Master Ball  15

**N**
Noctowl  11

**P**
Poké Balls  14-15, 27
Pokémon Trainers  6

**Q**
Quaxly  26-27

**R**
Rock type  24-25
Rotom Phone  18-19
Roy  14, 19, 25

**S**
Skiddo  12-13
Slugma  23
Snarl  7
Spinel  6
Sprigatito  21
Sudowoodo  24
Sunflora  10

**U**
Ultra Ball  15
Umbreon  7

**V**
Venomoth  13

**W**
Water type  22-23
Wild Pokémon  12-13

#  Quiz

It's time to find out how much you have learned! Read the questions and then check the answers with an adult.

1. What gives Sunflora energy?
2. Does Umbreon have a battle move called "Snarl"?
3. Can a Rotom Phone be used to identify Pokémon?
4. Is Slugma a Water-type Pokémon?
5. Which Pokémon was Dot's first ever catch?

1. Sunshine  2. Yes  3. Yes  4. No, it is a Fire type  5. Quaxly